BEHOLD THE HARVEST

A Guide for Laity

Pathway
P·R·E·S·S
CLEVELAND, TENNESSEE 37311

ISBN: 0-87148-442-0
Library of Congress
Catalog Card Number: 90-61073

Copyright © 1990
PATHWAY PRESS
Cleveland, Tennessee 37311

INTRODUCTION

What does our Lord want the Church of God *to be*, *to say* and *to do* in the next 10 years—1990-2000?

Three basic scriptural directives come into focus:

1. *He wants us to be* His representative, His voice, His agent—through the church—in every city, state and country around the world.

2. *He wants us to say* that His son, Jesus Christ, is the answer to the problems of life, the true source of peace and the hope of the future.

3. *He wants us to do* His work with an enlarged vision, renewed commitment and super enablement through the Holy Spirit.

How can we best accomplish these tasks in the next decade? Does God have a pattern, a course of action He wants us to embrace?

We feel God has impressed us to adopt the theme *Into the Harvest* and to bring the church together to respond to this challenge through Bible study courses, discipleship training programs and churchwide outreach projects.

The essential point of emphasis is togetherness to channel and combine our strength for God's glory to touch the world and to make a difference. This is God's call. And we are responding.

This *Guide for Laity* provides an overview of *Into the Harvest*, the commitment of the Church of God for the '90s. Subthemes for each General Assembly period are also listed. In this volume the 1990-92 subtheme "Behold the Harvest" is highlighted. The emphases for the two years are set forth and special programs, activities and resource materials are listed.

As you study this guide, the following pointers will assist you:

1. Prayer, worship and Bible study will undergird every emphasis and project we sponsor. For the past four years we have centered on these imperatives, and we will continue to do so.

2. Each two-year period will focus on a particular aspect of the harvest—"Behold the Harvest," "Laborers for the Harvest," "Reaping the Harvest," "Caring for the Harvest" and "The Spirit of the Harvest." Naturally, elements of each theme will be interwoven throughout all the ministries and activities of the church each year.

3. Special resource materials will be prepared to support and nurture the general theme and each subtheme. The materials are undated, however, and can be utilized by a local church at any time depending on need, schedule and growth patterns.

The Church of God is America's first Pentecostal denomination. We have a holy and beautiful heritage. Together, as we go *Into the Harvest* in the '90s in the power of the Holy Spirit, God will give us unprecedented growth, both spiritually and numerically. This is His plan for us. We will embrace His plan.

Executive Committee
Church of God

Table of Contents

1

Into
THE
Harvest

Introduction

As the Church of God approached its centennial celebration in 1986, three vital questions surfaced among church leaders.

Question 1: What were the strengths which had made the first hundred years of our church significant and noteworthy?

Question 2: Where did the Church of God stand at that moment in relationship to those strengths?

Question 3: What was to be the future for the Church of God?

In seeking to answer the first of these questions, thoughts centered on a noteworthy religious heritage, resulting in much emphasis on this theme at the Centennial Assembly in Atlanta.

As leaders pondered the other two questions, however, viable answers were more nebulous and complex. A special committee was appointed and these men came up with the Project 2000 theme, also introduced at the Atlanta Assembly and viewed today as the plan for where we should be going during the decade of the '90s.

Much of the work done by the Project 2000 committee dealt with candid evaluation of present strengths and weaknesses. Out of this evaluation and historical retrospection evolved 10 basic ministry goals which have now become familiar to most of our people through emphasis in our "Bold New Vision" and Discipleship '90 programs.

Implementation

While there was little if any disagreement on the 10 themes or areas of ministry emphasized in Project 2000, church leaders *did* discover it was more difficult to structure an instrument through which those goals and objectives could be realized. Out of their struggle to create a simple but viable procedure for implementing Project 2000, they returned to the Great Commission of the New Testament and crafted a 10-year emphasis which builds on the general theme *Into the Harvest*.

Project 2000

Centrality of God's Word
To appropriate God's Word as the criterion for all church ministries and personal living

World Evangelization
To reach the whole world with the gospel of Jesus Christ

Ministerial Development
To develop ministers for maximum efficiency in declaring the gospel and strengthening churches

Discipleship
To nurture believers in spiritual growth and personal development

Lay Ministry
To motivate lay witness and ministry participation in all believers

Biblical Stewardship
To establish believers as stewards of God's provisions in keeping with biblical principles

Church Growth
To implement the expansion and outreach of local congregations in ministry to contemporary needs

Church Planting
To plant churches in the fulfillment of the Great Commission

Family Enrichment
To challenge families to live by the authority of God's Word and to implement its values into everyday situations

Servant Leadership
To promote and build scriptural leadership models at every level of church organization

Not only was *Into the Harvest* the theme of our 1990 General Assembly, when Church of God delegates gathered in San Antonio in August, but this will be the continuing theme for all our church planning and promotional programs during the decade.

The subthemes for *Into the Harvest* and the upcoming General Assemblies are:

1990-92
Behold the Harvest
John 4:35

1992-94
Laborers for the Harvest
1 Corinthians 3:9

1994-96
Reaping the Harvest
Psalm 126:6

1996-98
Caring for the Harvest
1 Corinthians 12:25

1998-2000
The Spirit of the Harvest
Matthew 9:38

The driving force of the church *has been* and *must remain* godly compassion for and untiring efforts to win the lost of our world. Apart from the summation statement of the Great Commission (Matthew 28:19,20), there is little rationale for the church of our Lord Jesus Christ to exist. Yet within the scope of this commission, there are many facets of human life to which the gospel of Christ speaks and upon which the Holy Spirit works with powerful and revolutionary results.

While recognizing the centrality, the inerrancy, the absolute authority of God's Word, and while understanding that *evangelization of the world* is the phrase which best sums up our commission, we also acknowledge the miracle of Christ's abiding presence (Matthew 28:20) and the power of His Holy Spirit within us (Acts 1:8) to impact personal relationships, social and charitable institutions, and even the concepts by which free men construct laws and govern themselves.

It is within this broader definition of the Great Commission that we define our objectives, without apology, in terms of discipleship, family enrichment, ministerial development, lay ministry, church planting, biblical stewardship, church growth and servant leadership; and it is equally within these broad perspectives that we structure a strategy for thrusting every member of the Church of God *Into the Harvest* during the closing years of this century.

With this emphasis, we make no attempt to glamorize the year 2000, nor would we intend even to hint that the year 2000 has any scriptural significance. We wish to highlight the urgency of the hour, to capitalize on the present moment, to make use of our opportunity for reaching this generation with the gospel. Jesus reminds us, "The night cometh, when no man can work" (John 9:4), and the Scriptures reiterate, "Behold, now is the accepted time; behold, now is the day of salvation" (2 Corinthians 6:2).

Those who structured the decadal emphasis *Into the Harvest* realized full well that the Lord may return at any moment. We know not the day nor the hour of His return, but we know our responsibility to go into the whole world with the good news of salvation.

We also believe a long-range, decadal emphasis will assist all church leaders—international, state/provincial, and local—to participate in a united thrust of the church. We unite in the development of a strategy for progress, and we pray that, through the power of His Holy Spirit, those spiritual enemies which would hinder us will be routed and this church will come to the beginning of a new century with renewed strength and in revival power that will shake the strongholds of Satan as never before.

As a denomination we desperately need mature

Goals for
Into the Harvest

Recruit and maintain an international prayerforce of 500,000 laity and clergy

Lead 3 million souls to Christ and to the baptism in the Holy Spirit

Bring 1 million believers into church membership and biblical participation in the body of Christ

Involve 1 million individuals in a structured program of discipleship training

Send forth 5,000 ministers and missionaries for servant leadership in the harvest

Plant and establish 5,000 new missions and churches throughout the world

believers, men and women who understand the realities of spiritual warfare and who boldly stand forth to engage the Enemy. We need praying partners to hold up the arms of our leaders. We need strong families to undergird the moral values of our society. We need new churches within our cities. We need growing churches to inspire our communities. We need as never before a concerted effort to win the lost; and we believe we can develop it through a decade of emphasis on *Into the Harvest*.

In a certain dramatic sense, this could become for our church a real decade of destiny. What we are as we move into and through the next 10 years—our evangelistic fervor, our doctrinal purity, our spiritual balance, our breadth and correctness of vision—will impact and perhaps determine what we will be for many years into the future. Our thought patterns, our operational procedures, our communication tools, our openness to suggestions, our willingness to adapt—these too will shade and temper our impact upon a new generation, so we must strive to make that impact positive and worthy of our religious heritage.

We truly believe the Church of God, the oldest Pentecostal church in America, has a divine mandate from the Lord. We believe this church was called, structured and raised up for a purpose and that the role we have played up until this moment has been significant in terms of the Pentecostal revival sweeping our world.

More important, however, is a conviction that the best years are yet ahead for this church. There are greater victories to be won. There is more, much more, to be done; and we are determined to be faithful to "that heavenly vision" God has entrusted to us.

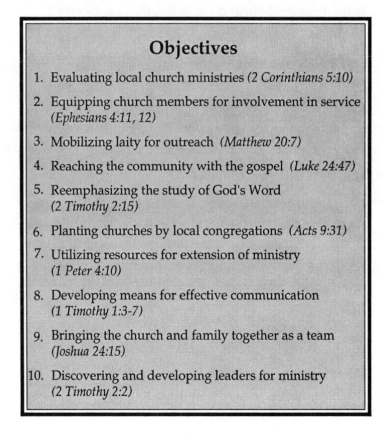

Objectives

1. Evaluating local church ministries *(2 Corinthians 5:10)*

2. Equipping church members for involvement in service *(Ephesians 4:11, 12)*

3. Mobilizing laity for outreach *(Matthew 20:7)*

4. Reaching the community with the gospel *(Luke 24:47)*

5. Reemphasizing the study of God's Word *(2 Timothy 2:15)*

6. Planting churches by local congregations *(Acts 9:31)*

7. Utilizing resources for extension of ministry *(1 Peter 4:10)*

8. Developing means for effective communication *(1 Timothy 1:3-7)*

9. Bringing the church and family together as a team *(Joshua 24:15)*

10. Discovering and developing leaders for ministry *(2 Timothy 2:2)*

Church leaders understand that the real battlefield, that place where true spiritual warfare is waged, is the local church, the local congregation. The general church structure exists primarily for the purpose of providing support material, backup, supplies for the local battle.

Some favorable signs are evident. Many of our churches have hired additional staff members. Others have expanded facilities, formed new outreach ministries and shored up areas that were weak.

Into the Harvest will emphasize over and again the responsibility of every church member to become involved. Souls are at stake. People are in need. Though society teeters on the brink of hell, at the same time undreamed-of opportunities are unfolding before our eyes.

During each of the next two-year periods, church leaders will share with all members different projects, activities and materials. These will be designed to bring the church together—nationwide, worldwide. There should come to all of us a greater sense of oneness, trust, security and a clearer understanding of the direction God's Spirit would have us travel.

We are each leaders in this fight. We are obeying the Lord Jesus Christ, and we are working together for His common cause, the lost of every race, color and creed. This knowledge should foster a stronger faith in us and in our children. It should and it must inspire us to greater sacrifice, and it will lead us to ultimate triumph.

Our Lord said, "I will build my church; and the gates of hell shall not prevail against it" (Matthew 16:18).

2

BEHOLD
THE
HARVEST

Harvest Declarations

Behold the harvest! Jesus commands it. The harvest reveals the very heart of God. It portrays the Great Commission.

Jesus spoke often about the harvest. It was one of His favorite topics. Usually He emphasized a plentiful crop, a need for workers and the priority of prayer. Four of His declarations emphasized key features that we should behold concerning the harvest.

First, the harvest reveals the plan of God (Mark 4:26-29). Man scatters seed. Night and day, whether the sower is asleep or awake (even if he does not know what is happening), the seed sprouts and grows. It produces an orderly result: first the stalk;

next the head, then the full kernel in the head. Finally, it requires reaping, putting the sickle to the grain because it is ripe.

Second, the harvest reveals the passion of Christ (Matthew 9:37, 38). Matthew focused on the motivation of Jesus: "He was moved with compassion" (9:36). His intense love for the lost exploded into a cry for laborers to enter the harvest.

Third, the harvest reveals the price of obedient service (Luke 10:3). In this declaration the focus is on discipline. In the previous chapter (Luke 9:23-26) Jesus had shown the cost of discipleship. In this chapter, 70 disciples were given strict guidelines for their mission into the harvest. The Great Commission commands, "Go ... teaching them to observe all things whatsoever I have commanded you" (Matthew 28:19, 20). There is a price to be paid in discipleship. Only a disciplined witness gives credible testimony.

Fourth, the harvest reveals the peril of the times (John 4:34-37). The focus of this declaration is on the urgency of the harvest. As Jesus and His companions traveled through Samaria, it was the time for planting. They watched farmers sowing seed in their fields. When the disciples returned from Sychar with food for their hungry Master, they found Him ministering to the woman at the well, with an overriding appetite for the work of the Father. He urged them, "Lift up your eyes, and look on the fields; for they are white already to harvest." A whitened harvest is in danger of being lost. To tarry is to lose the crop.

Harvest Examination

"Behold the Harvest" is the theme of the Church of God for 1990-1992.

A harvest field is not invisible. We cannot harvest what we do not see. "Son of man, what do you *see?*" was God's continuing question to the prophet Ezekiel before He revived a field of dry bones. Before Ezekiel could answer the question "Can these bones live?" he had to sit down "in the midst" of the valley of dry bones and "behold" the potential harvest.

Knowledge is power. What we see, said Jeremiah, affects our hearts (Lamentations 3:51). Knowing more about the harvest motivates us to reap it.

The local church needs people who know the trends and events in the community, the nation and the world. These are people who can see the finger of God pointing to a ripened, receptive harvest. They can see the finger of God in the social movements of our time, and in every story of human need. They can see the finger of God in demographic information that describes the population around them. They can see the finger of God through community groups who call attention to social needs.

Without vision, people will perish. Take time to see the harvest. Look on it intently with compassion and you will begin to see ways in which to reach your whitened harvest.

Harvest Evaluation

The early church beheld the harvest clearly, and began to reap it effectively. On the Day of Pentecost in Jerusalem, 3,000 were won to Christ (Acts 2:41). A short time later, thousands more were added (Acts 4:4). Soon the growth was so rapid that "the number of the disciples multiplied in Jerusalem greatly" (Acts 6:7). The church was growing in all the known world.

In early years our church experienced dramatic growth. We have continued to grow, but not always at the same high rates. Some local churches grow more rapidly than others. Some do not grow at all.

Early success was effected by the freshness of our anointing, the eagerness of our witness and the genuineness of our testimony. There is always a danger that our experience may grow cold and that we may lose our first love. We must maintain a fresh anointing.

Success was enhanced by our ability to communicate with our target population. We brought the gospel to friends and neighbors who were very much like ourselves. We spoke their language and fit well into their culture. Even in the industrial states, we were reaching the migrants from our home regions and our churches were growing rapidly.

On the mission fields, where growth continues to be spectacular, the most effective evangelism is by nationals who reach their own people and by foreign missionaries who have adapted to the local culture.

In most of our communities the target populations have become more diverse. There are probably some groups we have never reached well. Migrant populations we once reached so well have so blended into their new settings that they are no longer the same. If we do not recognize the change, we may retain methods and programs which no longer appeal to those we are trying to reach. In some cases we may even fail to reach our own children because they have been born into a new culture and are part of the new populations.

The opportunity for evangelism is as great as it ever was. People today still need Christ, and they will respond to the claims of the gospel. Paul gives us the plan for success: "I made myself servant unto all, that I might gain the more. . . . I am made all things to all men, that I might by all means save some" (1 Corinthians 9:19, 22).

The gospel does not change, but our manner of presenting it must be appropriate to our target population. We must learn to speak so that people will listen and respond. We are surrounded by people who need the gospel.

Our world has witnessed a population explosion of unprecedented numbers. Thousands of these young people have grown up without a true sense of moral values. They have been victimized by the worst influences in our society, but they are searching for something that is real—something that can make an eternal difference in their lives. One-third of our members are part of this generation and are able to reach their own.

Parents are looking for a spiritual environment in which they can bring up their children. They want help in teaching the things that really matter. In a recent survey, parents said that the youth ministry was an important reason for visiting the church the first time, and 94 percent said the youth ministry was an important reason for staying in the church. By ministering to the young we are able to reach whole families.

The elderly of our world provide another vital target population. For the first time in our history, there are as many people over age 65 as there are under 18. Often the elderly are lonely, ill, poor or dying. They need the help and fellowship of the church. To be ready for living and for dying, they need Christ. In every local church we have energetic and devoted members who are approaching retirement age. They can reach those of their their own age with the gospel.

Many of the church's target populations differ from our own. We must minister to various races, nationalities and cultures around the world and to those pockets of people who come to the United States. Some 25 million Hispanics live in the United States, and their number is growing. Migration from the Middle East has reached such proportions that Muslims outnumber Presbyterians.

Those who are different from us also need the gospel. We can reach them when we deliberately seek to understand them. Paul said: "Unto the Jews I became as a Jew, that I might gain the Jews; to them that are under the law, as under the law, that I might gain them that are under the law; to them that are without law, as without law, (being not without law to God, but under the law to Christ,) that I might gain them that are without law. To the weak became I as weak, that I might gain the weak: I am made all things to all men, that I might by all means save some" (1 Corinthians 9:20-22).

We must behold the harvest, and what we see must make a difference in what we do.

Harvest Attitudes

Have we beheld the harvest? Have we been moved by what we have seen? Are we ready to embrace those around us who need Christ?

The survey on the next page will help you see your church's attitude toward the diverse harvest.

Harvest Action

The next five chapters focus on specific areas of the harvest (note titles in diagram). The last two chapters deal with outlining programs, activities and steps of action to accomplish goals. At the end of each chapter you will find a section titled "Resource Materials/Special Activities." Only the name of the materials and activities are listed. The pastor will provide additional information about the nature, purpose and time frame of each project. In some instances the material will not be ready until the date listed beside it. If a date is not listed this denotes the material is presently in stock at Pathway Press.

Behold the Harvest in the Family
Behold the Harvest in the Church
Behold the Harvest in the Workplace
Behold the Harvest in the City
Behold the Harvest in the World

HARVEST ATTITUDE SURVEY

Show how the descriptions below apply to your local church by choosing one of the following responses:

A for always   **S** for sometimes
U for usually   **N** for never

_____ 1. Socialize with people of different ethnic groups

_____ 2. Have business contacts with people of different ethnic backgrounds

_____ 3. Invite new people to church

_____ 4. Feel comfortable with strangers

_____ 5. Enjoy new and different experiences

_____ 6. Live in racially mixed neighborhoods

_____ 7. Are comfortable around handicapped people

_____ 8. Have special training in dealing with the handicapped

_____ 9. Like to try doing things a new way.

_____10. Believe there are any number of ways of doing the same thing

_____11. Enjoy singing the same songs every Sunday

_____12. Accept a wide range of dress as appropriate

_____13. Speak more than one language

_____14. Like to travel or read about other cultures and countries

_____15. Welcome strangers to the church

_____16. Enjoy a variety of preachers and teachers

_____17. Are willing to commit funds to making the sanctuary and classrooms easily accessible to the handicapped

_____18. Have the time and resources to help newcomers to the community

_____19. Have a commitment to the poor

_____20. Commit time and resources to helping the poor

BEHOLD THE HARVEST IN THE FAMILY

The Bible Emphasis on Family Responsibility

Of all the volumes ever written, the Bible is the world's greatest champion of the family. From the description of the first family in the Garden of Eden to the description of the bride of the Lamb in Revelation, family imagery pervades the Word of God.

Even when man sinned, God showed the strength and beauty of the family by choosing to bring salvation to the world through the family. Through the seed of the woman, God promised to bruise the head of the Serpent. For centuries Jewish mothers cherished their children, fully believing that one day the Messiah would be born who would save the world.

The Savior was born, "made of a woman" (Galatians 4:4). God came to earth through the family of man. When Deity wrapped Himself in human flesh, the son of an earthly mother, He demonstrated for all eternity the marvelous glory of family.

As God spoke and revealed Himself to mankind, He did not limit His relationships to individuals. He entered into relationships with families. While it is true that every individual must know God personally, the great covenants established between God and the human race were with whole families. Rather than establishing His covenants with individuals God made covenants with the families of the earth, in much the same manner as when He covenanted with Eve and her seed.

Even though the Scripture says it was Noah who "found grace in the eyes of the Lord" (Genesis 6:8), God saved not only Noah but also his wife, their three sons and their wives. After the Flood, God said, "Behold, I establish my covenant with you, and with your seed after you" (Genesis 9:9). This was God's covenant with the family of humankind that never again would He destroy the world with a flood (Genesis 9:10-17).

God's covenant with Abraham was that He would become a great family, or nation, in whom all the families of the earth would be blessed (Genesis 12:1-3). Later it is recorded, "In the same day the Lord made a covenant with Abram, saying, Unto thy seed have I given this land" (Genesis 15:18). After Abraham offered God his son Isaac, God said, "I will multiply thy seed as the stars of the heaven, and as the sand which is upon the sea shore; and thy seed shall possess the gate of his enemies; and in thy seed shall all the nations of the earth be blessed" (Genesis 22:17, 18).

In a similar manner, the Mosaic covenant, the Palestinian covenant and the Davidic covenant were all established with the family and not just with the individual prophet, priest or king. Likewise, the writer to the Hebrews reminds us that the new covenant of Christ is "with the house of Israel" (Hebrews 8:10).

Throughout all of these scriptural examples, the family's acceptance of God's covenant implies also the acceptance of family responsibilities. God said of Abraham, "For I know him, that he will command his children and his household after him, and they shall keep the way of the Lord, to do justice and judgment" (Genesis 18:19).

When God gave the law to Israel, He said, "And these words, which I command thee this day, shall be in thine heart: And thou shalt teach them diligently unto thy children, and shalt talk of them when thou sittest in thine house, and when thou walkest by the way, and when thou liest down, and when thou riseth up. And thou shalt bind them for a sign upon thine hand, and they shall be as frontlets between thine eyes. And thou shalt write them upon the posts of thy house, and on thy gates" (Deuteronomy 6:6-9).

Christians today have a right to believe our sons, daughters, spouses, parents, siblings and extended family members will be a part of the great harvest of these last days. Peter's message is still relevant: "Repent, and be baptized every one of you in the name of Jesus Christ for the remission of sins, and ye shall receive the gift of the Holy Ghost. For the promise is unto you, and to your children, and to all that are afar off, even as many as the Lord our God shall call" (Acts 2:38, 39).

Hope for Every Family Member

There are two biblical truths Christians must remember in order to fully see and reap the harvest in the family. First, every person, including each loved one, is born into sin. Second, it is God's will to save every person.

Every person is born into sin. The psalmist said, "Behold, I was shapen in iniquity; and in sin did my mother conceive me" (Psalm 51:5). Paul explained that all humans sinned and died in Adam's transgression against God: "In Adam all die" (1 Corinthians 15:22).

Furthermore, because of this sinful nature that

has been passed on to each descendant of Adam, when every person is old enough to understand what is right and what is wrong, each one will sin. There is no family good enough to keep a child out of sin. There is no training guaranteed to steer a boy or girl away from sin. The sinful nature will over-power every person born into this world. As Paul said, "All have sinned, and come short of the glory of God" (Romans 3:23). This includes our family members.

It is God's will to save every person. When God gave His Son to die for the sin of the world, He did not exclude one soul. As Isaiah said, "All we like sheep have gone astray; we have turned every one to his own way; and the Lord hath laid on him the iniquity of us all" (Isaiah 53:6). As Peter explained, the Lord is "not willing that any should perish, but that all should come to repentance" (2 Peter 3:9).

Behold the harvest of the family!

Jesus said, "Lift up your eyes, and look on the fields; for they are white already to harvest" (John 4:35). This harvest field begins in the family. It would be tragic to go to the uttermost parts of the earth without first going to our own families "in Jerusalem."

Parents should remember, just because a son or daughter chooses to sin does not make them bad parents. Every son and daughter will choose to sin at some point in life. God is not unfaithful because of a child's choice, and a parent is not "bad" because of a child's choice. Parents, rather than berating themselves, should remember the fatherhood of God and that He is pleased for parents to pray on behalf of their children. Every son and daughter needs to know God's forgiveness.

The work of Jesus is "good enough" to save every soul. When John the Baptist saw Jesus the day after His baptismal service, he said, "Behold the Lamb of God, which taketh away the sin of the world" (John 1:29). While the expression "taketh away" is not totally inaccurate, it can be misleading to readers in the English language. It does not mean that He takes away sin from the life of every human. If that were the case, none of us would ever sin. But all human beings do sin, including children, spouses, parents, and brothers and sisters.

John used the word *airon*. It means "to raise up, to take upon oneself and carry what has been raised, to bear, to carry off" (*Thayer*).

When Jesus went to Calvary, He took up and onto Himself every sin of every human. He bore every sin—including every sin your loved one has committed or ever will commit—into the presence of the eternal Judge. When the Father Judge saw that sin—every one of those sins—He pronounced judgment: "Thou shalt surely die." On that day Jesus died and went to hell for every sin of the human race. As He went to hell, He carried every sin of your loved ones. In that sense, He "took away the sin of the world."

Was this sacrifice sufficient to save each one in your family? The resounding answer from the Word of God is YES. Isaiah said that when the Lord "shall see of the travail of his soul, . . . [He] shall be satisfied" (Isaiah 53:11). The sacrifice of Jesus on Calvary was "good enough" for the sin(s) of your child, your spouse, your parents, your brothers, your sisters and every member of your extended family.

What the Church Must Do

Let the church understand the family life cycle. No family remains the same over a period of time. Every "family of procreation" changes as it enters into the various stages or phases of its life. The church needs to understand where the family is in the life cycle in order to know how to minister.

Aldus and Hill listed seven stages of the family life cycle:

1. The establishment stage (parents' age about 22, first year of marriage)

2. The child-bearing stage (24-30 years old, married 2-7 years)

3. School-age children (31-37 years old, married 8-14 years)

4. Adolescent (38-44 years old, married 15-21 years)

5. Launching (44-52 years old, married 22-29 years)

6. Postparental (52-65 years old, married 30-43 years)

7. Aging (66-72 years old, married 44-50 years).

According to most studies, marital satisfaction in the average American family begins to decline after the first year and reaches its lowest level during the launching stage, when the couple has been married 22 to 29 years and they are from 44 to 52 years old. Many refer to this time as the empty-nest syndrome.

The church must understand what is going on in that family if a spouse is converted during this phase of low marital satisfaction. Naturally, a church is going to hear first from the spouse that has been won to the Lord and might be tempted to write off the unconverted spouse. However, one more change in a home at this critical stage may be enough to cause the unconverted spouse, already discontented with the marriage, to determine to pack up and leave. The church must understand these dynamics if it is to reap the harvest of the entire family.

Let the church understand the family as a system. To reap the harvest of the family, the church must know more about the family than the names, ages and addresses of the various family members. A family is not just a group of individual members. A family is more like a system.

When something happens to one member in the family, it has an impact on the entire family system. We should try to come to an understanding of how every member in the family feels. As strange as it may seem, when just one person in a family is converted, the family itself may become even more dysfunctional than before. If the entire family is to be reached, love and compassion will have to be extended to every member of the family.

There are many different types of needy and dysfunctional families that are white for the harvest. But for an example, let's consider the family in which a member who has been an alcoholic gets saved. Remember, "If you live in a typical American community, one out of six families in your neighborhood is affected by alcoholism" (Claudia Black). What is the effect of the conversion upon that family system?

For a family to function with an alcoholic member, the entire system must adapt. According to Sharon Wegscheider, an author and therapist who also grew up in a home with an alcoholic, there are six potential roles in such a home: (1) the dependent addict, who is motivated by shame; (2) the enabler, who is motivated by anger; (3) the hero, who is motivated by inadequacy and guilt; (4) the scapegoat, who is motivated by hurt; (5) the lost child, who is motivated by loneliness; and (6) the mascot, who is motivated by fear.

If the church is to win the family members of the converted alcoholic, it must do more than say to them, "Now you should be thankful because God has delivered your family from its problem of addiction." The family problem is more complicated than the chemical addiction. The church must also understand and minister to the anger, inadequacy, guilt, hurt, loneliness and fear of the other family members in order to reap that harvest.

In some ways, every family is like the alcoholic family. Different members will adapt their lives to fit in with other family members so the system will work. If the church understands this, it can reach the harvest of the families, because it understands the need of each family member.

Let the church minister the gospel in love. This is such a simple principle that it almost seems too trite to mention. However, if unsaved members of Christian families are asked why they do not serve God, the answers will almost always include the ideas that the church's demands are too hard and/or that in some way they have been hurt by someone in the church. Therefore, to reap the harvest of families, the church must fulfill the task of ministering the gospel in love.

First, the message of the church must be *gospel*. The word simply means "good news." If the message of the church is not good news, then neither is its gospel. It is not enough to simply inform people that they are sinners and if they do not repent they will go to hell. Neither the story of sin nor the truth of hell is good news. It is terrible news. The gospel is that Jesus died for sin and God forgives. The gospel concerning hell is that the believer does not have to go there. Therefore, let the message of the church be the gospel that brings salvation and not merely a message of the law, which brings judgment.

Second, the good news must be given in love. God is a loving Father. Jesus said that we should love one another even as He has loved us (John 15:12). If the gospel message is love, Paul explained that it will suffer long and will be kind (1 Corinthians 13:4). True love will bear all things, believe all things, hope all things, endure all things (v. 7). Regardless of what a family member may do, the church must have good news that is sent with a heart of love.

Steps for Reaping the Family Harvest

1. Suggest a family project in which each family draws a family tree beginning with the generation of the oldest living member. Indicate, perhaps by color highlighting, those who are known to be saved or

unsaved. Develop a strategy within the family whereby each member can be contacted personally about salvation by a Christian relative or concerned church member.

2. Establish care groups to minister to family needs within the church. Support groups to minister to the following needs should be considered: alcoholic families, victims of child or spouse abuse, premarital counseling, divorced people, children of divorce, homosexuality, grieving families, families of prison inmates, and so forth.

3. Begin or expand the church library to include books that address family issues, as well as books on evangelizing family members. The library should include books written for children on topics which often trouble them. These books can be used as the basis for talks between adults and children.

4. Conduct special family services and other family activities at regular intervals.

5. Keep family needs in mind in church schedules.

6. Address the sins of judgmentalism, bigotry and hate in sermons and in the Christian education ministry.

7. Develop strategies to reach unchurched families based on the question "How can our church help this family?" rather than the question "How can this family help our church?"

How Does Your Church Minister to Families

Use the appropriate number to denote how you feel your church ministers to families in your congregation and community.

0. No ministry in this area   3. Average ministry
1. Inadequate ministry   4. Good ministry
2. Weak ministry   5. Excellent ministry

1. Does your church provide resources for families, such as books, films and family-worship ideas?

2. Does your church provide premarital counseling for young couples?

3. Does your church provide activities in which three or four generations may participate?

4. Does your church provide worship services where the whole family worships together?

5. Does your church provide worship services for the different age groups?

6. Does your church provide a support group for families with an alcoholic member?

7. Does your church provide a support group for families with broken marriages?

8. Does your church provide a support group for families with "prodigal" children?

9. Does your church provide a support group for families with an unsaved spouse?

10. Does your church provide a support group for abusive families?

11. Does your church have regular prayer for unsaved family members?

12. Does your church endeavor to reach the unsaved family members of the children and teens in your Sunday school?

13. Does your church provide support services for battered women, abused children and unwed mothers?

Goals and Resource Materials

Special resource materials have been prepared to help achieve the goals highlighted in the section below. The materials are listed under the goals. They will be explained by the pastor and can be ordered from Pathway Press.

> **Recruit** and maintain an international prayer-force of 500,000 laity and clergy
>
> Lead 3 million souls to Christ and to the baptism in the Holy Spirit
>
> Bring 1 million believers into church membership and biblical participation in the body of Christ
>
> Involve 1 million individuals in a structured program of discipleship training
>
> **Send** forth 5,000 ministers and missionaries for servant leadership in the harvest
>
> **Plant** and establish 5,000 new missions and churches throughout the world

1. **Discipleship '90 Program**--Adults, Youth and Children
2. **The Church and Family Loyalty Campaign** "I Love My Church" (September 1991)
3. **Family Emphasis Video**--"Keeping the Family Together...In the Home and in Heaven"
4. **Church Covenant to Win Families**

BEHOLD THE HARVEST IN THE CHURCH

The Mission of the Church

But you are a chosen generation, a royal priesthood, a holy nation, His own special people, that you may proclaim the praises of Him who called you out of darkness into His marvelous light; who once were not a people but are now the people of God (1 Peter 2:9, 10, *NKJV*).

Before these words were addressed to the church, they were addressed to Israel. And the church, like Israel, has been chosen of God to be a light of salvation to the unsaved.

As the people of God, the mission of the church is to show forth, proclaim or announce to the world the praises of Christ who has called believers out of the darkness of sin into the light of His love and life. This is the good news the unsaved need to know—that they too can pass from the darkness of sin into the light of Christ's love and life.

Beholding the harvest of souls in the church must begin with the recognition that the church is the people of God. And as the people of God, every member of the church is called of God to be a priest— a priest involved in gathering the human harvest. So to begin gathering the human harvest in the church, all of God's people need to be involved in making Christ known as Savior and Lord.

Where is the field of harvest for the local church? It lies partially within the immediate sphere of the church's influence. Those unsaved individuals who come to our church and seek our help are within this immediate sphere of influence. We must seek to bring these to Christ for salvation.

But the field of harvest for the church also lies within the extended sphere of the church's influence. Those who do not or cannot come to our church, we must seek to bring to Christ for salvation by outreach ministries, personal contacts and various other means of communicating the gospel to the public.

By making Christ known to the world as the Savior and Lord of mankind, the church proclaims His praises and fulfills its own mission as the people of God.

The Field

Visitors

The visitors in your worship service may be there for a variety of reasons. They may have moved to the community recently and are looking for a church home. They may be people with a special need who have come to the house of God in search of help. They may be unsaved who have come to learn the way of salvation. Friends may have invited them to come and as a courtesy to them they are there. Or it may just be that the Lord sent them your way and it is up to you to determine the reason. Whatever the case may be, what a challenge, what an opportunity!

Those who visit your church may come from very different backgrounds. Some may be rich; others may be poor. Some may be teenagers; others may be senior adults. Some may have a background in your denomination; others may have no religious background. Some may be familiar with your style of worship; others may not. Whatever the case, each of them offers an opportunity to reach out and touch lives for the glory of God.

The visitors who attend your church service should be treated as honored guests. This entails getting their name, address and telephone number. They should be recognized during the service. Since they have honored you with their presence for the service, you should honor them with a contact the following week either by card, letter, telephone or personal visit.

The church should be involved in contacting visitors. Such involvement can be encouraged along lines of age, occupation, residency or common interest. A contact by someone other than the pastor will have a positive impact.

The Unsaved

The Master expressed the objective of His ministry this way: "The Son of Man has come to seek and to save that which was lost" (Luke 19:10, *NASB*). Every church should share this burden. As Dr. Robert G. Lee said: "Fishing for folks —saving souls— is the greatest business in the entire universe. We must look upon this business of rescuing the unsaved as being as important as getting a doctor for a sick child when it is desperately ill, as serious a matter as getting out the fire department when the house is afire, as imperatively necessary as giving an antidote when poison is in the stomach."

We can accomplish this end by giving an evangelistic slant to every service. Even the service that is pastoral in nature can be concluded in a way that points sinners to Christ. Also, personal interest can be shown to the lost. Some people will not come to Christ in the church service, but through developing a friendship with them, you may be able to win them to the Lord. When you have won their confidence by the consistency of your life, you can then testify effectively to them of the Savior who makes that life possible.

Friends

Statistics show that most of the converts to Christianity are won by friends or because of friends. Having won the confidence of a person, it is easier to share what Christ means in a life.

In their book *The Master's Plan for Making Disciples,* Charles and Win Arn list several reasons why winning friends should have priority. They say that friends provide a natural network for sharing the good news of God's redemptive love because they are receptive. Reaching friends allows for unhurried and informal witnessing. There is natural support when the friend comes to Christ; therefore, the assimilation of the new converts into the church is easy and effective. When friends come to Christ, they tend to bring their entire family. Also, they provide a constantly enlarging source of new contacts because they have a circle of friends who are potential contacts for Christ and the church.

One of the greatest services a church can render to its members is to lead them to reach out to their friends and seek to bring them to a saving knowledge of Jesus Christ. Can you imagine the inner satisfaction of having not only won a soul to the Lord but of having won a friend to this marvelous way of life?

Children

One of the ripest fields of harvest any church has is the children of the community. Their hearts are tender and they are open to the good news of saving grace. They are also a means of reaching other members of the family. Ministering to children of non-church attenders can result in getting the family into church and eventually winning them to the Lord.

Dr. W. A. Criswell wrote: "It would be impossible to emphasize too much the importance of children in the life and destiny of the church. They are the only material out of which God makes his preachers, missionaries, church members and Kingdom workers. They are the race itself, the church itself and the redeemed of God itself, tomorrow. He is a wise pastor who takes time for their care and upbringing."

Youth

Young people are standing at an important crossroad in their lives. They are searching for direction. According to Anthony Campolo, they "are influenced by the dominant values of our culture. Three of the most pervasive values are success, consumerism and personal happiness." Recent events in Europe remind us that young people are a powerful influence in our world. The church must address those areas of need in their lives and lead them with love toward the cross of Calvary.

The harvest of youth is ripe. The church must respond to this great need.

Singles

A large segment of our population is single. For some singleness is a choice; for others it is a crisis. Some choose to be single for the freedom and independence it offers. Others are single because of the death of a companion or as the result of a divorce. Some singles just need to find fulfillment in life; others are searching for answers to the perplexing problems life has brought to them. The church can stand in the gap and offer hope and encouragement to this special group.

Adults are more likely to be single today than they were in 1970. In fact, the single population age 18 and over rose from 38 million in 1970 (28 percent of all adults) to 66 million in 1988 (37 percent). Six in 10 women and nearly eight in 10 men aged 20-24 had not yet married in 1988, compared with 36 percent and 55 percent respectively in 1970. Between 1970 and 1988, the proportions in the 25-29 age group tripled for women and more than doubled for men. For those in the 30-34 age group, the proportions tripled for both men and women (U.S. Bureau of the Census).

About 10 percent of the young men and women today will never marry in their lifetime. For those who do marry, a large number will divorce, and the surviving marriages will eventually end in widowhood. But though singleness is most often a temporary state, while they are single, people have a set of unique needs for public and private sector services: child care and economic equity for single parents, education and work opportunities for young adults, and housing and health care for the elderly are all associated with trends toward greater singleness in our society.

Young and Middle Adults

On July 1, 1987, the median age of U.S. citizens was 32.1 years, according to the U.S. Bureau of the Census. (There are as many people older than the median age as there are younger.) People aged 35-44 made up the most rapidly growing age group in the United States. About 3 of every 5 people are between the ages of 15 and 64, or 60 percent of people in the United States are between 15 and 64.

Those now reaching middle age comprise a more stable, serious and careful culture. This age group has been marrying and having children later in life and are slower to rediscover religion than those in previous generations--those who rejected religion as young adults, then returned to religious tradition after having children. They are also more educated, making them less likely to hold religious beliefs. But according to Cheryl Russell, religion will play a central role in the lives of most in this age bracket and in the social and economic choices made in this country in the next few decades.

The group in our society that is shrinking the fastest are those from ages 18 to 55. Still, they represent needs and must be reached for the Lord.

A good Sunday school class is ideal for reaching young and middle adults for the Lord.

Senior Adults

The fastest growing segment of society is the senior adults. There are more citizens 55 and above than there are teenagers in some Western nations..

Many senior adults are lonely and feel neglected. They need to know that someone cares about them. They know that their time is limited, and many have not made preparation for eternity. How rewarding it would be to show them the way to Christ so that their final years might be lived in communion with Him.

Outreach Opportunities

Three places almost every community has that are ripe for ministry are hospitals, nursing homes and jails.

What an opportunity the hospital offers. In these moments of crisis the church has a golden opportunity to demonstrate that it cares. A prayer, a verse of Scripture, a friendly word may lift a spirit and change a life. Your concern then may lead the patient to eternal life.

Nursing homes are filled with lonely people who need to know that someone cares about them. A visit, a service, a song may be just what is needed to meet the needs of one who is having a bad day.

In the jail you will meet people whose lives are out of kilter. Some of them will realize that they have missed the mark. These may be eager to find a better way. When you tell them about Jesus, He can change their lives. The fact that some prisoners use religion to gain release from jail is no excuse for not seeking to share Christ with all who will hear.

A jail service should center around Christ and the hope He offers mankind. In Him is every answer the human soul is seeking. By sharing this message publicly and privately, you can be used of the Lord to win some inmates to Him.

There are other means of reaching souls. Radio is an effective means of outreach. Many people still wake up to the sounds of the radio. Others tune in as they drive down the road. Some just have the radio on as they go about their housework. A church that offers a service tailored to its community will find an audience to hear its message.

Approaches to radio may vary. Some churches broadcast their Sunday morning worship service. A 15- or 30-minute broadcast can be effective. Even a five-minute devotional or inspirational program or a one-minute spot announcement can yield results.

The newspaper is also a good tool for bringing your church to the attention of the community. In a small community, almost everyone reads the weekly newspaper. An ad, an article, or a news item about your church is sure to get the attention of readers.

There is no more powerful means of communication than television. While this medium has been abused by some, it offers a challenge to those who love God and want to spread His Word. The cost may be prohibitive in some cases, but where a church can afford to televise its services or even offer spot announcements, the dividends can be tremendous.

Harvest in the Church

Questionnaire

1. In what ways does your church provide on-going training of laypeople to reap the human harvest?

2. In what ways does your church seek to make newcomers welcome and have them become members of the church?

3. In which of the following does your church conduct some type of outreach ministry? hospital_____ nursing home _____ jail/prison _____ other _____

4. Through which of the following media does your church seek to reach your community for Christ? bulletin/newsletter _____ newspaper _____ radio _____ television _____ other _____

5. Of the outreach and media ministries your church does not have, which do you think it would be practical for your church to begin?

6. What do you think would be a realistic goal for annual percentage increase in your church's Sunday school attendance? 2% _____ 5% _____ 10% _____ other _____%

7. Assuming your church could realize the annual percentage increase you chose in question 6, what would your church's Sunday school attendance be in the year 2000?

8. What are some things you think your church can do to attain the annual percentage increase in Sunday school attendance indicated by your answer to question 6?

9. How many people do you know personally in your community (both relatives and acquaintances) who are unsaved?

10. What are you doing to influence the unsaved people you know to come to Christ?

5

BEHOLD
THE HARVEST
IN THE WORKPLACE

Light on Monday Morning

"'You are the light of the world.... Let your light shine before men'" (Matthew 5:14, 16, *NIV*).

Sunday morning in church: Sunday school was good, the singing was uplifting, and you didn't even mind when they passed the offering plate. On a spiritual scale of 1 to 10, you felt like a solid 9.

Monday morning at work: Your boss is mad at the world, the fellow at the next desk is blowing cigarette smoke all over you, and your phone rings every three minutes. You feel just spiritual enough to be disgusted with the whole world.

What a difference a day makes! Only 24 hours earlier, nestled in the warm sanctuary of the church, your light was shining bright enough to guide ships at sea. Now, faced with the hassle of the workplace, you may not feel that you could outshine the bulb in the back of the refrigerator . . . but you can! You can because the same Holy Spirit that was in your life on Sunday morning is in your life on Monday morning. And He gives us real power to witness for Christ.

When Christ talked about taking up our cross daily (see Luke 9:23), He meant for us to make a full-time commitment to Him. That entails taking Christ with us into the workplace—directly into a turbulent world of deadlines, quotas and irate bosses. It means letting our light shine—living right and being a witness for Him—no matter how much aggravation the job brings.

Providing the light of the gospel in the workplace can be a tremendously rewarding experience even though, at times, it may seem like a difficult task. "'In this world you will have trouble,'" Christ said. "'But take heart! I have overcome the world'" (John 16:33, *NIV*). With such a powerful ally, we *can* be effective witnesses at work . . . even on a dreary Monday morning.

The Working World

According to the United States Department of Labor, there were 123.8 million people in the labor force in September 1989. Of that number, 117.5 million were employed full-time. The unemployment rate was 5.1 percent.

Women make up approximately 45 percent of the labor force. Latest figures show that the unemployment rate among women is 6.1 percent, somewhat higher than that for men.

While these statistics may vary for different parts of our world, there seems little question but that the number of married women who work outside the home has been increasing since World War II. Working mothers with children are having a significant influence upon the workplace.

What's the future of the workplace? Experts predict a number of trends and changes in the workplace over the next decade.

Change in the workplace. More people will work from their own home in the 1990s. With advances in computer technology and telemarketing, we are seeing a move toward what sociologist Alvin Toffler calls the "electronic cottage."

Increasing concern for job enrichment. Many workers are unhappy and feel alienated on the job. To combat these concerns, greater efforts will be made to enhance job enrichment and worker satisfaction.

Increase in democracy on the job. Following the lead of Japanese and European companies, American corporations will encourage employee participation in management decision making. The use of quality-control circles is likely to increase.

Changing work week. In the decades between the 1940s and the 1980s, the average work week dropped. Shorter work weeks mean more time for leisure activities.

As the occupational structure of society changes, the church needs to be informed and prepared to reap the harvest in the workplace. While the message of the gospel remains the same, the methods of communicating the message must be geared to the rapid changes taking place. These changes demand our most creative thinking as we become involved in the workplace all around the world.

Silent and Spoken Witness

If you're a full-time worker, you spend about 2,000 hours a year on the job. That's a big chunk of your life. Two thousand hours is far more time than you spend in church and probably more time than you spend with your family in an average year.

Whether we intend to or not, we're going to have an impact on our coworkers during those many hours. We simply can't spend that much time around people without making some sort of impression on them.

The Spirit-filled, witnessing Christian is paid a salary to preach the gospel in the marketplace. Think of it! Every day you can minister on the job, a place where the paid clergy cannot enter. We have the opportunity to impact our coworkers with our lives (silent witness) and our lips (spoken witness).

On-the-Job Evangelism

Although it may seem a long way from church, the workplace offers tremendous opportunities for telling others about Christ. Since our lives are a constant witness, we call this kind of witnessing *lifestyle evangelism*.

Simply put, lifestyle evangelism is not a *program* but rather the *process* of living out our Christian commitment day by day. Jesus said, "Ye shall be witnesses unto me" (Acts 1:8). Look closely at the word *be*—it refers not so much to *what we do* but *who we are*. Lifestyle evangelism is simply what we are—living out our lives as an open book reflecting the Christlife.

When it comes to the workplace, lifestyle evangelism has the added advantage of being a *long-term* process. With 2,000 hours a year at our disposal, we can get to know people and build real relationships on the job.

Lifestyle Evangelism

1. List two or three coworkers who have had an influence on your life. _____

_____

2. How have they influenced you? _____

_____

3. List two or three coworkers you have influenced. _____

_____

4. Tell how. _____

_____

_____

Presenting the Plan of Salvation

Ask helpful questions.

The following questions may be helpful in a spiritual discussion that flows naturally out of your relationship with that individual.

1. How would you describe your relationship with God?

2. At what point are you in your spiritual pursuits?

3. What do you think God expects from man-

kind?

4. If you were God, what requirements would you make for people to go to heaven?

5. If you were standing before the gate of heaven and God asked, "Why should I let you into heaven?" what would you say?

Share the Gospel

God's position. God *loves man* and wants to have fellowship with him. "For God so loved the world, that he gave his only begotten Son, that whosoever believeth in him should not perish, but have everlasting life" (John 3:16).

God's perfection. This means He cannot lower His standard without violating His character. "'Therefore you are to be perfect, as your heavenly Father is perfect'" (Matthew 5:48, *NASB*).

Man's condition. *All people have sinned* and fallen short of God's perfect standard. "For all have sinned and fall short of the glory of God" (Romans 3:23, *NASB*).

God, in His justice, requires the penalty of *spiritual death* (eternal separation from God). "For the wages of sin is death" (Romans 6:23).

God's provision. *Jesus Christ*, being God, paid the penalty for man's sins by dying on the cross as his *substitute.* He made it possible for man to have a personal relationship with God by offering His perfection in exchange for man's sin. "He made Him who knew no sin to be sin on our behalf, that we might become the righteousness of God in Him" (2 Corinthians 5:21, *NASB*).

Man's decision. All anyone must do is *trust in Christ* and His death *alone* as sufficient payment for sin. This satisfies God's requirement of perfection and establishes His desired eternal relationship with man. "But as many as received Him, to them He gave the right to become children of God, even to those who believe in His name" (John 1:12, *NASB*). "For by grace you have been saved through faith; and that not of yourselves, it is the gift of God; not as a result of works, that no one should boast" (Ephesians 2:8, 9, *NASB*).

Help Develop New Christians

Our desire is to help the new Christian achieve the following goals:

Walk in the Spirit. "But the fruit of the Spirit is love, joy, peace, longsuffering, gentleness, goodness, faith, meekness, temperance: against such there is no law. And they that are Christ's have crucified the flesh with the affections and lusts" (Galatians 5:22-24).

Worship regularly. "For where two or three are gathered together in my name, there am I in the midst of them" (Matthew 18:20).

Grow in Christ. "Be careful for nothing; but in every thing by prayer and supplication with thanksgiving let your requests be made known unto God" (Philippians 4:6).

Share Christ. "Let the redeemed of the Lord say so, whom he hath redeemed from the hand of the enemy" (Psalm 107:2).

Care for others. "Then shall the righteous answer him, saying, Lord, when saw we thee an hungred, and fed thee? or thirsty, and gave thee drink? When saw we thee a stranger, and took thee in? or naked, and clothed thee? Or when saw we thee sick, or in prison, and came unto thee? And the King shall answer . . . Inasmuch as ye have done it unto one of the least of these my brethren, ye have done it unto me" (Matthew 25:37-40).

Travel heavenward. "Be thou faithful unto death, and I will give thee a crown of life" (Revelation 2:10).

Lifestyle Evangelism Pointers

The goal we should keep in mind is to help coworkers more clearly understand the message of the gospel so they can make their own decision based upon truth. Here are some excellent pointers to remember:

1. *Be consistent.* We witness by what we say and by what we don't say. Speaking well of others, always being truthful, not complaining or gossiping—all these make a powerful impact on others. The negative person who constantly complains is making an impression too, but it is the wrong impression.

2. *Be conscious of work time.* Use wisdom when it comes to witnessing on company time.

3. *Use tracts wisely.* These are an excellent way to witness, but use them with discretion.

4. *Know your coworkers.* Without being nosy, find out about their hopes and dreams and their family situation.

5. *Be helpful.* Little kindnesses done for coworkers make a favorable impression on them.

6. *Be competent.* Incompetent work or laziness will greatly detract from your witness. Be the best that you can be in doing your job.

7. *Use your testimony.* It is better than a "preachimony."

8. *Get involved socially.* Make your coworkers your friends by being around them in off-the-job functions.

9. *Don't argue.* Paul instructed Timothy, "Remind your people of these great facts, and command them in the name of the Lord not to argue over

unimportant things. Such arguments are confusing and useless, and even harmful" (2 Timothy 2:14, *TLB*).

10. *Learn to listen.* People are looking for those who care enough to listen to them without judging or giving advice. If you are a good listener, you will know when a person is hurting and you will be able to minister to that need.

Ideas for Reaching Coworkers

What are specific things we can do to reach co-workers for Christ? A few suggestions:

Be the best you can be on the job. Your attitude toward work makes a tremendous impression on those around you. If you move at half-speed, stretch coffee breaks and bad-mouth the boss, most people aren't going to be interested in the religion you profess to follow.

Use the workplace media. Does your company have a bulletin board? An employee newsletter? Perhaps you could use them to tell others about special events at your church.

Workplace medias are also ideal for advertising community service programs of your church, such as food banks, shelters for the homeless and disaster relief funds. Coworkers will be more receptive to you and your church if they see your congregation is active in helping others throughout the community.

Pray for coworkers. Pray for them as individuals with individual needs. Learning and praying about the specific needs of coworkers takes a lot more effort than a general "God bless everyone at work," but the rewards are great!

Pray for your company. Ask God to help your company compete honestly and well in the market-place. Pray that He will give good judgment to the men and women who lead your firm, and ask His blessings on your immediate supervisor . . . even if you have an unsympathetic person for a boss.

Be available. Tom spent breaks and lunch hours reading his Bible in a corner of the company cafeteria. Tom thought he was being spiritual. His co-workers thought he was overdoing it.

Try not to be a recluse on the job. Spend a few coffee breaks with your fellow workers, getting to know them as more than just faces on an assembly line. People need to know and trust you before they'll open up to you about spiritual matters. You'll have plenty of time for private devotions at home.

Keep a Bible handy. Look around . . . there may not be another Bible in your entire office or shop. Keeping a Bible on your desk creates a witness others notice, even when you're not there.

There is another reason to have Scripture at your fingertips. Sooner or later, a coworker will ask you to explain what you believe about God. Such an opportunity to defend your faith will almost always come when you're not expecting it, so it's good to have a Bible nearby. Pointing out specific Scriptures is always more effective than mumbling and making up verses as you go. Even if you don't have space for a full-size Bible in your work area, you can surely tuck a New Testament into your pocket or purse.

Start a workplace Bible study. This idea won't work for everyone, but if you have a gift for teaching, it can be an ideal way to reach people. Be sure to clear things with your supervisor before you launch your first meeting. Chances are, your company will have no problem with an on-site Bible study as long as it doesn't interfere with the normal flow of work.

Summing Up

Lifestyle evangelism is a good and natural thing; and because it is a long-term process, we can develop meaningful relationships with those who need Christ. Once our coworkers learn we're Christians, they will be watching every day to see if our walk is as good as our talk.

Albert Schweitzer said it well: "Example is not the main thing in influencing others. It is the only thing."

You already know the workplace can be a pressure cooker. With deadlines to make, quotas to fill and unreasonable customers to pacify, your job may be anything but spiritually uplifting. Sometimes witnessing can be the farthest thing from your mind.

But those times of greatest stress can also make the greatest positive impression on your coworkers. Let them see you exhibit grace under pressure—see you keep your cool when virtually everything goes wrong—and they're going to want what you have inside. The time will come when you'll be ready to "give an account for the hope that is in you" (1 Peter 3:15, *NASB*).

Work is one of the few places that gives us 2,000 hours a year to get to know people, love them and preach daily sermons with our life. The office or factory can be more than a place to earn a living; it can be the greatest harvest field we'll ever enter for Christ.

Goals and Resource Materials

Special resource materials have been prepared to help achieve the goals highlighted in the section below. The materials are listed under the goals. They will be explained by the pastor and can be ordered from Pathway Press.

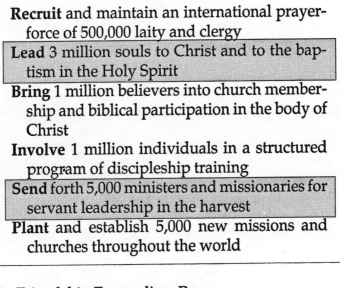

Recruit and maintain an international prayer-force of 500,000 laity and clergy

Lead 3 million souls to Christ and to the baptism in the Holy Spirit

Bring 1 million believers into church membership and biblical participation in the body of Christ

Involve 1 million individuals in a structured program of discipleship training

Send forth 5,000 ministers and missionaries for servant leadership in the harvest

Plant and establish 5,000 new missions and churches throughout the world

1. Friendship Evangelism Program
2. Lifestyle Evangelism Program
3. Evangelism Breakthrough
4. Women Reaching Women Program

6

BEHOLD
THE HARVEST
IN THE CITY

God Looks at the City

A church that senses a heartfelt burden for the lost people of its city shares the compassion of God who sent Jonah to the great city of Nineveh. Although Nineveh's thousands had apparently done nothing to warrant his mercy, He pitied them to the extent that He called an unwilling Jewish prophet, guided him on a reluctant journey to Assyria and commissioned him with an eight-word message ("Yet forty days, and Nineveh shall be overthrown" [Jonah 3:4]) that brought a citywide revival.

A church that seeks the salvation of unheeding, often hardened, neighbors shares the spiritual tenderness of Jesus, who wept over Jerusalem because of its residents' resistance to truth.

A church that ministers with the desire to see people in its community turn to God and have their lives changed is spiritual heir to Paul, who looked over Corinth and heard the voice of God's assurance: "I have much people in this city" (Acts 18:10).

There is a great harvest in the city. While the reference to "city" may stir images of skyscrapers, subways and slums, it intends to convey the idea that in whatever population center you live—in city or town or village, among hundreds or handfuls—a harvest of souls awaits your evangelistic action.

What is the spiritual profile of the place where you live and minister? The percentage of people who claim church membership varies from state to state, ranging from highs of over 60 percent in some southeastern states to lows around 40 percent in the northwestern area of the country. If a church is going to conscientiously minister to its surrounding population, it is necessary to investigate the spiritual temperature of the area.

All You Need to Know About Your City

The magnitude of the spiritual harvest in the city where you minister can be determined by a demographic survey. Demography is the study of vital statistics of a population. A lot of information about communities is available at little or no charge, but churches rarely know of its existence and do not often take advantage of it.

Most towns have a City (or County) Planning Commission, which uses census data as a base for preparing maps, charts and tables giving character-istics of the community. Their maps show how many people live in each census tract (usually a several-block-square area). Charts indicate the family size, race, household income, educational level and other useful factors.

This information can be cross-referenced to data about churches, also available from local govern-ment agencies. In the absence of a planning commis-sion, similar profiles can be obtained from the Cham-ber of Commerce, public utility companies, public libraries, newspaper research departments, or nearby universities or colleges.

The benefits of such a survey may be demon-strated by the experience of one pastor in a city of 38,500 who discovered in a demographic study that his area had 71 churches, with a total seating capac-ity in all churches of 28,800 and an average weekly attendance of 17,710 at all churches. A quick calcu-lation (38,500 minus 17,710) revealed a potential har-vest of 20,790 unchurched individuals. If his church could win only one-half of one percent of the non-at-tenders, it would add 104 people to the congrega-tion!

A demographic survey can normally be completed in about 20 hours, and it will provide useful information.

Steps Toward Reaching Your City

After carefully considering the harvest potential in your community, it is important to begin specific planning. While the growth emphasis has a way of focusing on numbers, you must not lose sight of the fact that growth is the by-product and not the point of reaping God's harvest in the city. The church's purpose is not just to expand its membership rolls; it is to bring the message of Christ to a world that is suffering and helpless. The church is a refuge and training ground, a loving, caring alternative to an impersonal and self-serving world. The following steps may help you focus the church's renewed efforts to reach the lost.

1. *Analyze your church's attitude toward the harvest.* Most churches believe that they want to reach the lost, but it is important to realize that this often means bringing in new people with different backgrounds and ideas—different ways of worshiping, different styles and different heritages. What is the church's attitude toward those who are different? (The Harvest Attitude Survey reproduced in chapter 2 is helpful for measuring attitudes.) The harvest is as diverse as the kingdom of God is diverse. If the

local congregation is not ready for that, some preliminary work must be done in opening hearts and eyes to the need to embrace those who are different.

2. *Analyze the harvest in your community.* Your church should name a task force of responsible men and women who will conduct a demographic study as defined above and supplement it with their own knowledge and impressions of the community, using the resulting information to answer questions about spiritual needs. Are the elderly fully served by local congregations? Is there any evangelism among teenagers? Is there a new immigrant population nearby? Is outreach needed in housing projects?

3. *Determine your best target population.* Based on your survey data, decide where evangelism is most needed and how you are capable of ministering. Two truths should guide you in the process. First of all, do not be hesitant to admit that the absolute best prospects for evangelism are the people in your community who are most like the people in your church. In employing your evangelistic strategy, understand that people who are very different from you will not accept your message as readily as those who are most like you.

A second truth, which balances the first one, is that people who are different from you—whether the difference is educational, racial, economic or whatever—cannot be reached by people like themselves if there are no Christian people like themselves in the community. Their only hope is cross-cultural evangelism. We usually reserve the term *cross-cultural* to identify racial, language or ethnic distinctions, but there is a very real sense in which other less obvious barriers must be crossed for local church evangelism to be successful.

4. *Develop a long-range plan for evangelism.* Goals should be flexible and should take into account probable changes in your community's demography during the coming decade as well as projected changes in your church. Consult individuals from all areas of your church's ministry for suggestions and information.

5. *Set specific, measurable short-range objectives.* Your long-range plan will be divided into phases and phase one should begin immediately. You know more about the present than you do about the future, so your immediate goals can be specific and directed toward a date. Make sure the objectives are measurable, and keep the plan flexible.

6. *Celebrate the plan and encourage the whole church to commit publicly to it.* The congregation should make a joyous, enthusiastic commitment to its evangelism plans, feeling a sense of God's guidance and blessing.

Finding the People Who Need to Find You

If a church is newly beginning, one approach to evangelism may be particularly effective. But if it is an already-established church, a different methodology is apt to be more productive.

New churches are successful in attracting new people by conducting a Community Needs Survey and then acting on what is learned from the responses. A sample form of such a survey is found in this book on page 84. Another similar strategy that gets the same information in a different way is a telephone survey. "Calling in Love," a training program for conducting a telephone survey which results in many new people attending the start-up services of a beginning church is identified at the end of the chapter under Resource Materials.

Established churches usually discover that their best prospects are the friends, neighbors, schoolmates, acquaintances and coworkers of the men and women who already attend the church. A ministry which challenges existing members to pray for their friends and relate to them in ways calculated to attract them to church may multiply the church's evangelism success.

A simple program can be devised by a local church without need for an extensive investment in materials. It would work like this: A dinner meeting is held at which the pastor explains how friendship evangelism works. He helps his people understand that the major source of new attenders in any church is the friendship/kinship network of those who presently attend. (National surveys reflect that 20 percent of newcomers arrive at the church for a variety of other reasons, but 80 percent come because they already know someone at the church.) Building on these facts, he challenges each church family to do the following:

1. Pray specifically and regularly by name for an unchurched acquaintance, someone outside the immediate household.

2. Agree in prayer with a brother or sister in the church, each of them mutually praying for the other's friend.

3. Seek ways to relate to the friend in nonchurch settings in order to build the relationship and strengthen friendship. This might involve inviting the friend for dinner, strategizing to spend time in activities that the friend enjoys (sports, shopping, etc.) or going places together.

4. Look for opportunities to introduce the friend to other church people, again in nonchurch settings.

5. Arrange for visits to church functions or activities outside of regular church services. This might include Bible study in a home, church music presentation, children's activity, sports function, church

picnic, and so forth. This step begins to acclimate the unchurched person to the church environment, but in a nonthreatening way.

6. Prayerfully seek an opportunity for the friend to hear a presentation of the gospel. This might be done personally, by a mutual friend who has evangelism skills or in a church service.

7. Once a positive response to the gospel is made by the friend, continue a relationship that helps him or her become established in the church.

This approach to friendship evangelism can be strategized by a churchwide emphasis that plans and schedules special activities ("seeker sensitive") designed to attract and minister to the unchurched.

An excellent resource for Christians who want to relate meaningfully and spiritually to the unsaved/unchurched is Joseph Aldrich's book *Gentle Persuasion*. Another useful book is Win Arn's *The Master's Plan for Making Disciples*.

The Absolute Best Way to Win People

It has been demonstrated that the most effective way to win new people is by establishing new churches. Numerous reasons undergird the truth of this claim.

The growth curve of the majority of churches shows an upward climb for the first 10 years, then a plateau for the next 10-20 years, followed by a gradual downward turn. The earliest years of a church are the most fruitful for winning people.

Most communities which have not seen the birth of a new church in the past 10 years are ripe for a harvest.

Another practical reason for starting a new church is that people simply like different kinds of churches. Rather than fighting this idea and trying to press people into a mold of "our kind of church," it is more effective to permit the existence of different kinds of churches in the city. This does not call for theological or doctrinal difference; merely cultural difference that recognizes, for example, that some people like one type of music and some another. (Strange as it might seem, such personal preferences often affect church choices more than doctrinal distinctives!) Let us multiply churches in the cultural mosaic in which we live and minister.

What often happens when an existing church takes the initiative to start a church in a nearby community, giving a nucleus of people for the purpose, is that the new church succeeds and the vacuum created by those who leave is soon filled with newcomers, the existing church quickly growing again to its previous size or even larger.

Some of the best new church starts in our movement have come as the result of the efforts of laypeople burdened to reach new people and blessed by their pastors to proceed with the labor.

COMMUNITY SURVEY

Use this form, or your adaptation of it, in a house-to-house survey in your area. It will help you become acquainted with the perceived needs of a community and at the same time help you become acquainted with the people who live there. Using the findings of the survey, you can design programs of your church which will minister to the community and consequently attract people.

1. Are you an active member of a church in this community?

2. In your opinion, what is the greatest need in this community?

3. Why would you say most people don't attend church?

4. What do you think would attract people to a church here?

5. We're starting a new church here. What advice would you give to pass on to our church leaders?

6. May I mail you some information about our new church? (Get address.)

Goals and Resource Materials

Special resource materials have been prepared to help achieve the goals highlighted in the section below. The materials are listed under the goals. They will be explained by the pastor and can be ordered from Pathway Press.

Recruit and maintain an international prayer-force of 500,000 laity and clergy

Lead 3 million souls to Christ and to the baptism in the Holy Spirit

Bring 1 million believers into church membership and biblical participation in the body of Christ

Involve 1 million individuals in a structured program of discipleship training

Send forth 5,000 ministers and missionaries for servant leadership in the harvest

Plant and establish 5,000 new missions and churches throughout the world

1. Church Growth Emphasis--seminars, conferences, programs
2. Media Campaign, *Your Answer, Jesus Christ*
3. "Calling in Love" Telephone Campaign
4. Nationwide Visitation Campaign (1992)

7

Behold
the Harvest
in the World

Our Worldwide Challenge

The entire world is the church's harvest field. This is clearly stated by Jesus in His commission to the church (Matthew 28:19, 20). The Great Commission outlines the basic framework of the church's missionary assignment. The church is to preach the gospel in all the world for a witness to all nations. Every nation, tribe and tongue is to hear the good news of the salvation of God in Christ Jesus.

The church's responsibility for reaching its world is reiterated at the ascension of Christ when He said, "But ye shall receive power, after that the Holy Ghost is come upon you: and ye shall be witnesses unto me both in Jerusalem, and in all Judaea, and in Samaria, *and unto the uttermost part of the earth*" (Acts 1:8).

In the Book of Acts, the apostles are seen at work, first as missionaries to their own people and later as ambassadors of Christ to the nations of the world. The missionary significance of the outpouring of the Spirit at Pentecost is beyond human estimation. The fledgling church spread its wings in the power of the Spirit and carried the message of salvation to the farthest reaches of its world. Retrospectively, Mark wrote, "And they went forth, and preached every where, the Lord working with them, and confirming the word with signs following" (Mark 16:20).

The world's population now stands near 5.4 billion (1990). Experts predict that at the present rate of increase, the total will reach 7 billion by the year 2000.

An estimated 2.7 billion people have no effective Christian witness and therefore do not have the opportunity to know about Jesus. About 2,000 language groups still need Bible translations. Compounding the challenge of the harvest, approximately 1 billion illiterate people can know of Jesus only through personal evangelism or audiovisual ministries.

The church is God's appointed instrument for preaching the whole gospel for the whole man to the whole world. If the church fails to preach God's way of forgiveness of sins, no one else will. Thus, the world will remain in sin, separated from God. Christ's commission does not spell out all the duties of the church in this world or the total mission of the church. It concerns itself primarily with the outreach of the church into the world of nonchurched people, whoever and wherever they may be. The emphasis, therefore, is to make disciples and to evangelize the nations until the total world has had the opportunity to hear the good news of salvation.

The Church and the Harvest

The missions areas of the Church of God are experiencing dramatic growth. Reflecting the dynamic activity of the Holy Spirit throughout the world, numerical increases have been extraordinary.

Under the impetus of the Holy Spirit, new fields are opening to the church.

A Growing Harvest

In areas where the Church of God is already established, the harvest continues:

- The growing church in Indonesia, with 253,513 members, is experiencing a tremendous revival. They have set themselves the ambitious goal of reaching a national membership of 5 million members in 10,000 local churches by the year 2000. The largest congregation in the Church of God, with 18,000 members, is found on the island of Java in the city of Surabaja. This dynamic church is presently enlarging its sanctuary to seat 20,000 worshipers. Two other Indonesian congregations, one in Jakarta and a second one in Surabaja, each have more than 5,000 members.

• The Word for the World Fellowship, a Church of God ministry in the Philippines, now has more than 10,000 members. Even though they have constructed a 2,000-seat auditorium in Manila, they still must have multiple worship services to accommodate their growing membership.

• Membership in Guatemala now stands at 90,000, up from 20,000 just 12 years ago.

• Nicaragua has established 233 churches since the Sandinistas came to power in 1979. The total is now 325 churches.

• Forty-three new churches have been organized in the Dominican Republic since the 1988 General Assembly.

• A Church of God in Panama had 2,000 converts in a recent crusade. Attendance, now 1,500 each Sunday, is growing rapidly.

• Despite severe persecution by the former government of Bulgaria, the Church of God in that country has continued to grow. The church is now registered and permitted to erect buildings.

Humanitarian and Social Concerns

Evangelism has always been and remains the first priority of the world missions outreach of the church. However, a total ministry requires ministering to physical and social needs as well as the spiritual needs of people.

Hundreds of elementary and high schools, 72 Bible institutes and colleges, several seminaries and dental and medical schools are operated in missions areas by the church. More than 9,000 national students are now being trained in Bible schools. Hungry people are fed, and medical and dental treatment are provided through clinics located in several countries.

The church also directs Volunteers in Medical Missions (VIMM), an interdenominational Christian organization composed of doctors, dentists and health-care professionals who are interested in using their skills to reach the lost for Christ. VIMM's president is a Church of God medical doctor.

With funds received through the annual Christ's Birthday offering and special appeals, the church ministers to disaster victims in missions areas.

Mission Churches Involved in Missions

For most of the history of the church's world missions outreach, the churches in the United States and Canada have borne the major share of responsibility for missions personnel and support. Now, as our churches mature in many countries, they are assuming the task of supplementing the missions effort by themselves providing personnel and financial support. The Philippines, Guatemala, South America, Germany, Africa and England now send and support missionaries to other countries. The Word for the World Fellowship, a Church of God ministry in the Philippines, now sends and supports missionaries to Australia, Hong Kong and Singapore. The German church has had a 36 percent increase in missions giving and now provides full support for three missionary families and partial support for another.

Actions for Local Church Involvement

(Money, Projects, Activities)

Open Doors for Harvest

Momentous changes are occurring in the world. Communist countries that once were difficult or impossible to enter have become a major harvest area in this decade.

In the vast Soviet Union, *perestroika* (restructuring) and *glasnost* (openness) are bringing about fundamental changes. Dramatic changes in the countries of Eastern Europe such as Poland, Hungary, Czechoslovakia, Bulgaria, East Germany and Romania present new opportunities for the church in the 1990s.

Doors of opportunity for evangelism exist in Indonesia, the Philippines, Central America, South America, Africa and other areas of the world.

The entire world is the mission field of the church. Just as the early church was led into new fields by the Spirit, we need to be prepared to follow the leading of the Spirit as new opportunities are presented in decade of the '90s.

Organize a Missions Committee

Your church can be stimulated to growth in its missions interest and involvement if a few people commit themselves to making a concentrated effort on behalf of missions in the church. The local missions representatives and the missions committee with the cooperation of the pastor are the key force for missions activity and promotion in the church.

The objectives of the local missions committee are to bring together all the church's missions activities and prepare one master program, to establish and maintain a program of missions awareness in the church throughout the year, and to promote each aspect of the missions program.

The organization of the committee can vary according to the size and the structure of your church. If the committee is small, each member may have several areas of responsibility. If the committee is large, each member will probably have only one or two duties.

Resource materials. The missions department can provide the local missions committee with a wide variety of resource materials for missions involvement. These materials include books, brochures, flash-card stories, dramas, children's programs, posters, tapes, area maps, 16mm films, filmstrips and videos. Some items are free. Films are loaned at no charge.

To receive a complete listing of resource materials and an order blank, write: Church of God World Missions, P. O. Box 2430, Cleveland, TN 37320-2430.

Following are some ways the local missions committee can raise the level of missions interest and involvement in the local church.

Educate for missions. A balanced program of missions involvement should include missions education that involves all aspects of church life: Sunday school, Family Training Hour, worship services, the music program, boys and girls activities, youth groups, Ladies Ministries, Men's Fellowship, vacation Bible school, summer camp, and other educational groups.

The primary responsibility for the success of missions education in the local church lies with the pastor and the local missions committee.

Establish a missions interest center. A missions interest center in your church will inform and stimulate the members. It could be a bulletin board in the foyer on which you display maps, posters, pictures of missionaries and other eye-catching materials. Or you could set up a missions room containing, in addition to the above mentioned items, artifacts, books, videos and other items of missions interest.

Conduct a missions conference. The harvest involvement of your church can be enhanced by the development of an annual World Missions Conference.

Establish, first of all, the objectives you wish to achieve through your missions conference, whether it is one service or extends over several days. The following objectives are given as examples:

• To encourage a greater missions awareness through exposure to missionaries and nationals from the field

• To encourage a greater missions awareness through indirect exposure to the mission field

• To so present the needs of missions work that there will be a deliberate response by the people in prayer and giving.

The local church missions conference should be planned and promoted by the local missions committee with the cooperation of the pastor.

Summary

The world missions outreach of the Church of God is now 80 years old. A look back through the years staggers the imagination to consider just what God has accomplished through this church. From a halting start by R. M. Evans, a retired Methodist minister recently filled with the Holy Spirit, the church's outreach has evolved into a worldwide ministry. As we enter the final decade of this century, a great harvest of souls awaits the church's efforts in the fields of the world. The Great Commission gives us the responsibility for preaching the gospel to all the world. Along with Christ's commission, we have His assurance that He will be with us always as we accept the challenge of world evangelization and go into the harvest.

Goals and Resource Materials

Special resource materials have been prepared to help achieve the goals highlighted in the section below. The materials are listed under the goals. They will be explained by the pastor and can be ordered from Pathway Press.

> **Recruit** and maintain an international prayer-force of 500,000 laity and clergy
>
> **Lead** 3 million souls to Christ and to the baptism in the Holy Spirit
>
> **Bring** 1 million believers into church membership and biblical participation in the body of Christ
>
> **Involve** 1 million individuals in a structured program of discipleship training
>
> **Send** forth 5,000 ministers and missionaries for servant leadership in the harvest
>
> **Plant** and establish 5,000 new missions and churches throughout the world

1. *Decade of Destiny*--A strategy for World Missions
2. A complete listing of support/promotional materials is available from the World Missions Department, P.O. Box 2340, Cleveland, TN 37320-2430.

8

BEHOLD
THE HARVEST
AND ACT

A Biblical Mandate for Action

An effective principle for action is expressed in the simple phrase *"Plan* your work and *work* your plan. No plan will work unless you do."

The work of the church often suffers from the lack of planning. It also suffers from failure to act on the planning. Dreams may be good starting points, but they are not enough. Strategies and plans must be effectively implemented if the mission is to be realized.

To motivate and encourage ourselves into the action phase of the harvest, let us consider the following points and passages.

Action Is an Acknowledgment of the Lordship of Jesus (Luke 6:46)

Jesus raised this probing question: "'Why do you call Me "Lord, Lord" and do not do the things which I say?'" (Luke 6:46, *NKJV*). In the words that follow this question, Jesus proceeds to describe the person who hears his words and does them. The outcome of the action is the ability to withstand the storms. The strength of the foundation is the sayings of Jesus, acted upon. His words, spoken and heard, are not sufficient. Only when the spoken words are acted upon is the foundation secure.

Action Is a Key to Happiness (John 13:17)

This passage comes from the context of the Lord's Supper and the washing of the feet of the disciples. The principle embraced is a universal one. Blessings and happiness come not from the knowing but from the doing. In fact, knowing brings indictment and condemnation in the absence of action. Jesus is our teacher and He is our Lord. His commandments are to be joyfully and explicitly obeyed. The mandate for action on the part of His servants arises from the example He sets. "I am your Lord and master; I have done this, therefore you are to do it!"

Action Is the Fulfillment of Personal Ministry (Luke 12:48)

Acting on spiritual knowledge expands one's capacity for service. It also enhances the reward factor when the books are balanced on Judgment Day. Accountability is based on the extent to which one knows. This does not mean that "ignorance is bliss." A close look at Luke 12:48 reveals that those with limited knowledge will be chastised. It should be observed that we have a responsibility to know. Willful ignorance does not exempt us from judgment and subsequent punishment. Punishment is the inescapable negative side of inaction. We have a vested interest in avoiding that.

The positive side of action is the joy of knowing that our Lord is pleased with what we have done about the knowledge He has imparted. One huge lesson to be learned from all of this is that action is nonoptional for believers. Action is optional to the extent that we are free to do or not to do. But it is not optional if Jesus is truly our Lord and Master. We cannot continue in disobedience and expect His favor. Disobedience is the original sin. James tells us that it is a sin to know to do good and fail to do it (James 4:17).

Action Is the Confirmation of Our Faith (James 2:14-26)

The Faith Chapter (Hebrews 11) reveals that all the heroes of faith were people of action. Abraham believed and acted out his faith. Rahab is cited by James and by the author of Hebrews as an example of faith that moved to action. God spoke to Noah about a flood and an ark. Because Noah believed what God revealed, he built the ark exactly as the Lord instructed.

Failure to act out our faith brings disaster to others, as well as self-destruction. One trembles at what might have been had Noah, Abraham, Moses and others only "mouthed" their faith. And what about Jesus? What would the future be like if Jesus stopped with merely uttering His love for the world? He laid down His life as a demonstration of His obedience to His heavenly Father and to confirm His love for the world. What will we do?

The Process of Action

The biblical mandate to act in view of the vast soul harvest is unquestionable. The words came from Christ himself and have been echoed down through the centuries by those who were consumed by evangelistic zeal to reach souls for the Lord.

Plan Wisely

Purposes and goals point directions. Priorities help leaders choose which goals are most important. Planning is the thrust that converts goals into action and dreams into reality.

Planning must be based on measurable, realistic goals. It is not always easy to define clearly what goal is to be accomplished, but the failure of many plans can be attributed to unclear goals. If goals are clear and can be clearly communicated, they will attract clear and communicable plans.

Establish Prayer Groups

The need for prayer should be evident. As local church leaders prepare for the harvesting of souls, there can be no greater source of strength than that which comes through prayer.

Establishing prayer groups can come about at the beginning of meetings when three or four can pray for specific needs. Also, prayer retreats can be valuable in giving individuals time to get to know one another and become a team to pray together. Or people can meet at various homes for times of prayer.

Encourage Creativity

New ideas that will generate enthusiasm and

bring about desired results are always welcomed by leaders. No one person has all the worthwhile ideas and strategies to get the work done. But together new thoughts can be sharpened and readied for use. Encourage each person to be creative and innovative as the harvest thrust is considered. Always remember that when an idea is presented, it becomes the property of the group to refine and use.

Delegate Responsibility

A basic reason for delegating responsibility within the context of the church is that it is biblical. Moses was counseled by Jethro to divide the work with other men (Exodus 18). Also, delegating responsibility is necessary to get the task completed.

Some guidelines for delegating responsibility are as follows: (1) Choose qualified people, (2) exhibit confidence in the person, (3) make duties clear, (4) give authority to make decisions, (5) set up controls, and (6) give praise and credit for the work.

Give Authority

Responsibility without authority does not work. Jesus gave his disciples responsibility. He also gave them the power to accomplish the assignment. Responsibility is easier to share than authority, but both are necessary.

Require Accountability

The effectiveness of delegation can be increased by clear lines of accountability and procedures to follow. When the person to whom responsibilities are delegated knows he will be accountable to a group or leader, he can plan wisely, keep a record of actions and evaluate step-by-step so essential changes can be made.

Recognize Achievements

Offer praise, credit and recognition when the delegated task is successfully completed. Such recognition will make individuals more willing to accept unusual and heavy responsibilities. Give thanks to God for both the accomplishments and the servants who become channels through whom the Lord acts.

Six Areas for Local Church Action

The harvest reveals the very heart of God and draws us into action by the admonition of Christ that we behold the harvest and act.

Consider the harvest areas you have studied and use the following form to write down steps of action that your church will take.

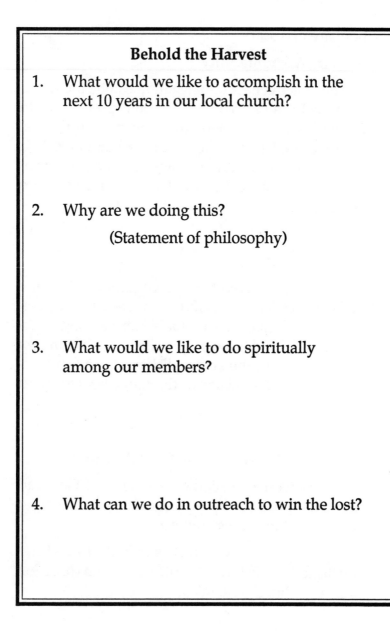

Behold the Harvest

1. What would we like to accomplish in the next 10 years in our local church?

2. Why are we doing this?

    (Statement of philosophy)

3. What would we like to do spiritually among our members?

4. What can we do in outreach to win the lost?

5. What can we do to improve and enlarge our facilities to accommodate an increase in attendance?

6. What can we do about additional paid staff to help with ministry?

7. What can we do about finances? What budget should we set?

8. What are some other areas we must consider?

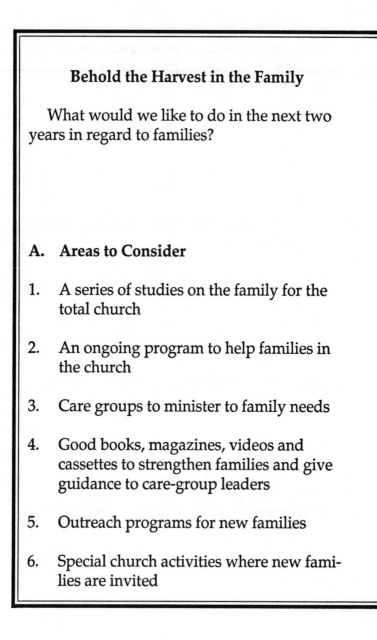

Behold the Harvest in the Family

What would we like to do in the next two years in regard to families?

A. Areas to Consider

1. A series of studies on the family for the total church

2. An ongoing program to help families in the church

3. Care groups to minister to family needs

4. Good books, magazines, videos and cassettes to strengthen families and give guidance to care-group leaders

5. Outreach programs for new families

6. Special church activities where new families are invited

7. Family prayer groups

8. Help for the homeless and underprivileged in the community

9. Other areas

B. Plan of Action

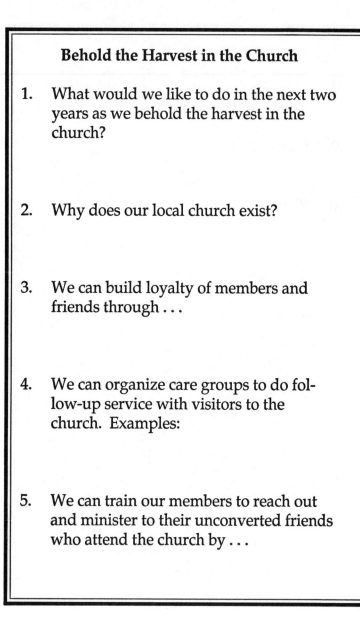

Behold the Harvest in the Church

1. What would we like to do in the next two years as we behold the harvest in the church?

2. Why does our local church exist?

3. We can build loyalty of members and friends through . . .

4. We can organize care groups to do follow-up service with visitors to the church. Examples:

5. We can train our members to reach out and minister to their unconverted friends who attend the church by . . .

6. Children provide us great opportunities to reach parents. Some plans could be . . .

7. We can reach unchurched children in the community through the following programs:

8. We can minister to the unfortunate in hospitals, nursing homes and jails through the following programs:

9. Our goal for increased Sunday school attendance in the next two years will be . . .

10. Our goal for Family Training Hour attendance in the next two years will be . . .

11. We can increase our financial program through stewardship training such as . . .

Behold the Harvest in the Workplace

As we reflect on the harvest in the workplace, we plan to do the following during the next two years:

1. We will design a program to train church members and friends in the opportunities and know-how of reaching people in the workplace. An example might be . . .

2. We will organize prayer groups to pray for workers as they witness to unchurched colleagues and coworkers.

3. We will do a survey to determine how many workers are associated with a firm that has a newsletter or employee media program.

4. When input to the newsletters and media programs are available, we will set a goal of reaching _____ people in the

workplace in the next two years.

5. When it is possible to start workplace Bible study, the church will do so and offer specific guidelines and materials, such as

6. We will train our members to know the *do's* and *don'ts* of witnessing on the job. Plans for this are . . .

Behold the Harvest in the City

What can our local church do during the next two years to reach unchurched people in the city?

Statement of Challenge

While the reference to city may stir images of sky-scrapers, subways and slums, it is intended to convey the idea that in whatever population center you live—city, town or village: among hordes, hundreds or handfuls—a harvest of souls awaits your evangelistic action.

What We Will Do

1. We will secure demographic information to help us understand the areas we will penetrate.

2. When possible, we will work through the ministerial association in relationship to other denominational efforts that are under way.

3. We will provide ongoing training to assure an adequate team to work in the city outreach efforts.

4. We will utilize the media--radio, newspaper and television--to reach the city. Plans call for . . .

5. We will study our potential for reaching the city but will set a realistic goal of winning _____ people to our church in the next two years.

6. We will make adjustments in our facilities, budget, training program and social life to accommodate those won to the Lord. Such plans might include . . .

7. We will draft other plans as needed.

Behold the Harvest in the World

What can our church do about the harvest throughout the world?

Statement of Challenge
"Ye shall be witnesses unto me both in Jerusalem, and in all Judaea, and in Samaria, and unto the uttermost part of the earth" (Acts 1:8).

A. In keeping with our Lord's command, we will . . .
    1.

    2.

    3.

    4.

B. Our missions financial goal for the next two years will be _____. We intend to raise this amount through . . .

C. A special missions project will be established for the country of _____.

D. We will keep the ministry of foreign missions before our people through use of

E. We will organize missions prayer groups according to the following plan:

F. We will support the international YWEA program.

G. We will establish the following fund-raising project.

Conclusion

Commendation and reward comes from the Lord when His servants have been faithful to His command. He rewards faithfulness. How would you respond if the Lord should say, "Don't tell me how busy you were, just tell me what you have accomplished." Remember, "'That servant who knows his master's will and . . . does not do what his master wants will be beaten with many blows'" (Luke 12:47, *NIV*).

9

UNITY AND COMMUNICATION

New Emphasis for Our Church

If our decadal emphasis *Into the Harvest* is to succeed, it is altogether crucial that we maintain unity of purpose and establish well-defined lines of communication.

It is significant that leadership has already conceived, structured and gone public with a decadal emphasis theme. While *Into the Harvest* may not seem like something altogether new—its being but a reaffirmation of the Great Commission—it is at the same time the first goal-oriented proposal approved by the Executive Council and the General Assembly which spans the tenures of a number of General and State Overseers.

Into the Harvest offers opportunity for every level

of leadership—world and international, state and regional, district and local—to become acquainted with, and to buy into, the overall goals and objectives of the church. It permits time for themes and emphases to be built into Sunday school curriculum, thus getting into the classrooms where our children are first learning of the church's mission, and it gives opportunity for periodicals, news-letters and brochures to pick up on the themes and for pastors and local leaders to structure their programs within the same areas of emphasis.

Not to be overlooked, as well, is the fact that *Into the Harvest* will permit newly elected or newly appointed leaders to know from day one where the church is in terms of these long-range objectives. And it should make work immediately more effective, with less time demanded for gearing up and preparing to assault the strongholds of the Enemy.

How We Will Talk About Our Work

Properly defined, communications must be understood as dual-track. It means both giving and receiving information, both telling and listening. *Into the Harvest* is a program which cannot possibly survive unless we discover and maintain adequate communications tools. We must talk about our work. We must listen to one another. We must share ideas and profit from each other's successes and failures. Such a strategy will require open, honest, candid communication on every level. It will mean constant examination, analysis and evaluation. It may mean discarding ideas that are not working and instituting new concepts geared to a changing marketplace. It will certainly mean making use of the new technological tools for communication.

We know for certain there will be the need for input from the grass-roots level of our church. It is one thing to design battle plans but quite another to discover how effective those plans really are on the front lines. For this reason, it will be necessary to receive from local churches

- honest reactions
- candid information
- structured surveys
- personal and group testimonials
- shared success stories.

These will constitute some of the communications tools that will keep our varied units in touch with each other.

How We Will Share Ideas

There are at least four specific routes by which we will share ideas for *Into the Harvest:* (1) leadership communication, (2) the magazine *Youth and Christian Education Leadership,* (3) the denomination's official magazine, *Church of God Evangel,* and (4) more effective use of video- and audiotapes to give local churches a summary of materials.

Leadership communication

Beginning with announcement of the 1990 General Assembly theme, *Into the Harvest* has become and will remain a watchword of the church. You will see these words on stationery, posters, brochures, curriculum covers and in periodicals of all descriptions. *Into the Harvest* will be the theme at prayer conferences and other state and international gatherings, and it will appear more and more in local church bulletins and programs.

As the turbulent '90s unfold, leadership throughout the Church of God will be emphasizing and reiterating that the church's chief mission is *Into the Harvest.* It is a theme we hope every member and every person who attends our church will come to consider vital to our existence.

Youth and Christian Education Leadership

Plans call for this quarterly magazine to communicate the *Into the Harvest* message to youth and Christian education leaders in the local church. It is an ideal tool to achieve this goal. The announcement of materials, programs and ideas will be coordinated with the *Minister's Bulletin* so the pastor can work with his leaders as a team in understanding and fulfilling the goals of *Into the Harvest.*

This sharing progress will enable the goals of each subtheme to be emphasized, and it will keep workers abreast of what is taking place and how to be involved.

Youth and Christian Education Leadership will update promotions tools and materials for pastors and local church leaders. It will feature a working calendar, surveys, questionnaires, statistical information and shared innovative ideas from leaders around the world, thus becoming what we hope will be a utility vehicle for every local leader.

Church of God Evangel

Further changes are planned for the *Evangel,* America's oldest continuing Pentecostal magazine, in order to make it the premier communications tool of *Into the Harvest.*

The first and most important of these changes has to do with philosophy, for the *Evangel* will become more closely reflective of the Executive Committee's goals and objectives. This will be accomplished through the Executive Committee's more active participation in *Evangel* planning, the choosing of *Evangel* themes and the structuring of *Evangel* ads and other materials.

Through this official journal of the church, leaders will communicate directly with pastors, church clerks and local members, emphasizing *Into the Harvest* and highlighting each two-year theme of the decade.

Modern technology has teamed up with this new appreciation for the effectiveness of an official journal in order to make the communications task more effective. In January 1990 the *Evangel's* official lead time for articles was cut from the traditional 60 days to 30 days, thus making all materials in the magazine more current for the reader.

In addition to this, desktop publishing permits better use of drop-in pages such as "Church Update," printed at the last minute and capable of getting late-breaking news to the reader within seven to 10 days, almost as effective as and certainly more economical than the personal letter.

Not only is it hoped that the *Evangel* will become in essence as well as in name the official communications piece of the entire church but that, through the Board of Church Ministries and other strategy-planning sessions, the magazine will take on new life up front in the planning stages and new life out on the field in terms of its reception and increased circulation.

Specific efforts will be made to increase *Evangel* circulation through
• Renewed commitment to relevance and keeping in touch with what is happening in today's world

- Greater efforts to reflect the church's unique doctrinal and Pentecostal perspectives
- Official endorsement at all levels of leadership
- Direct contact with every pastor
- Direct contact with every church clerk
- Appeal to every local church leader
- Renewed emphasis on every church participating in roll subscriptions
- A goal of at least 20 personal subscriptions from each local congregation
- Efforts to modernize the mailing list.

Low-end or Inexpensive Video and/or Audio Presentations

These could be audio readings of *Evangel* or leadership articles or it could conceivably represent certain special issues of the *Evangel* itself on video—program materials condensed and quickly summarized for local workshop dialogue. It most certainly means that the church will stay abreast of those developing communications tools destined to become more pronounced during the decade of the '90s.

How We Will Develop, Produce and Distribute New Support Materials

Into the Harvest will require constant attention to support materials. These will be produced by the Executive Committee, under the auspices of the Executive Council and working through duly appointed boards and committees.

Support materials

• Designed with pastor and local church flexibility in mind

• Advertised early in the *Evangel* and *in Church Leadership*

• Made available on time and well in advance of needed deadlines

• Marketed at competitive prices

• Aimed at helping the local church minister more than at telling the local church what and how to minister

In addition to all this, there is likely to be more emphasis on use of FAX machines, computer disks, and computer telecommunications which will permit instant access to information and better immediate or overnight answers to inquiries.

Conclusion

With the entire world reshaping itself and with new and growing opportunities for ministry developing overnight, the decade of the '90s promises to be one of the most exciting chapters *ever* in the history of this church. We *must* make use of every ministry tool at our command, and we *must* enlist, train and deploy every person possible in the battle for lost men and women.

The leadership of this church is committed to do just that.

We invite you to join us in the fight.

Christ is our Lord—we give Him all the glory.

The world is our harvest field—we go forth in the name of Jesus and in the power of His Holy Spirit.

On the following page is a listing of our specific goals.

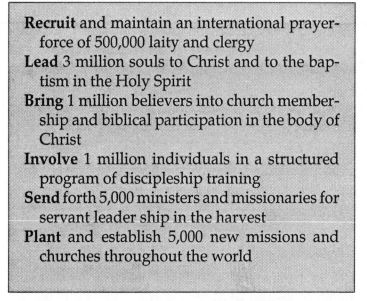

Recruit and maintain an international prayer-force of 500,000 laity and clergy

Lead 3 million souls to Christ and to the baptism in the Holy Spirit

Bring 1 million believers into church membership and biblical participation in the body of Christ

Involve 1 million individuals in a structured program of discipleship training

Send forth 5,000 ministers and missionaries for servant leader ship in the harvest

Plant and establish 5,000 new missions and churches throughout the world

We commit these goals to His divine providence, vowing as never before to pray and to labor for a harvest of souls.

> The Executive Committee
> Church of God
> Cleveland, Tennessee